SNL PRESENTS:
THE CLINTON YEARS

WRITTEN BY THE WRITERS AND CAST OF

SATURDAYNIGHTLIVE

COMPILED BY

MICHAEL SHOEMAKER
SCOTT WEINSTEIN

TV Books

NEW YORK

Library of Congress Cataloging-in-Publication Data
available upon request from the publisher.

ISBN: 1-57500-045-8

The publisher has made every effort to secure permission
to reproduce copyrighted material and would like to apologize
should there have been any errors or omissions.

TV Books, L.L.C.
1619 Broadway, Ninth Floor
New York, NY 10019
www.tvbooks.com

Interior design by Eric Baker Design Associates, Inc.
Manufactured in the United States of America.

From the moment

William Jefferson Clinton became a serious contender for the Presidency in 1992, the writers and cast of "Saturday Night Live" trained their attention on him.

Now for the first time, this collection of the best in SNL's coverage is presented in book form. From his first jogging steps on the presidential campaign trail through the sex and job scandals in the Oval Office, and up through the impeachment hearings of 1999, this treasury of Clinton humor is a keepsake for all fans of "Saturday Night Live" and all who laugh and cry at the political shenanigans in Washington.

COLIN QUINN

Question:

What do you get when you cross Joey Buttafucco with a college education?

Answer:

After "Dateline NBC"
aired the interview with
Jane Doe #5,
Juanita Broderick,

President Clinton was asked if he was a rapist. The President told reporters, **"It depends what your definition of 'ist' is."**

Today, President Clinton took a day off from dealing with NATO's bombing of Kosovo and spent it playing golf at Camp David. After his round, a refreshed President told reporters,

"You know, OJ's right. This game does take your mind off killing people."

At the White House this week, President Clinton officially came out against same-sex marriage.

What's more,

the President said he's

not too crazy

about opposite-sex marriage,

either.

In court documents made public this week, Independent Counsel Kenneth Starr told a federal judge that Hillary Clinton is now a

"central figure"

in the Whitewater criminal probe.

Reacting to the news, President Clinton called the investigation a "partisan witch hunt," vowing, quote, **"If the First Lady is somehow convicted and has to go to jail, I will do everything in my power**

to wait two weeks to start dating."

Our top story tonight:

As new questions arise about Hillary Clinton's role in

Whitewater,

the President appears to be distancing himself from the First Lady. Earlier today in his weekly radio address, the President insisted,

"Hey, I sleep with

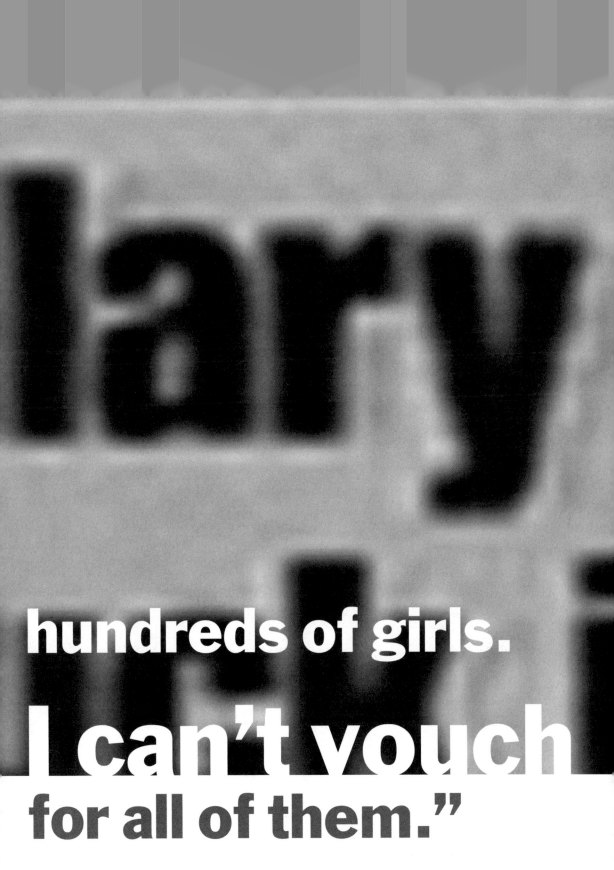

hundreds of girls.

I can't vouch for all of them."

Meanwhile, President Clinton is hard at work on Tuesday's State of the Union Address, in which he'll focus on crime, education, and the economy. At the request of the First Lady, part of the President's speech will be

huge

lies.

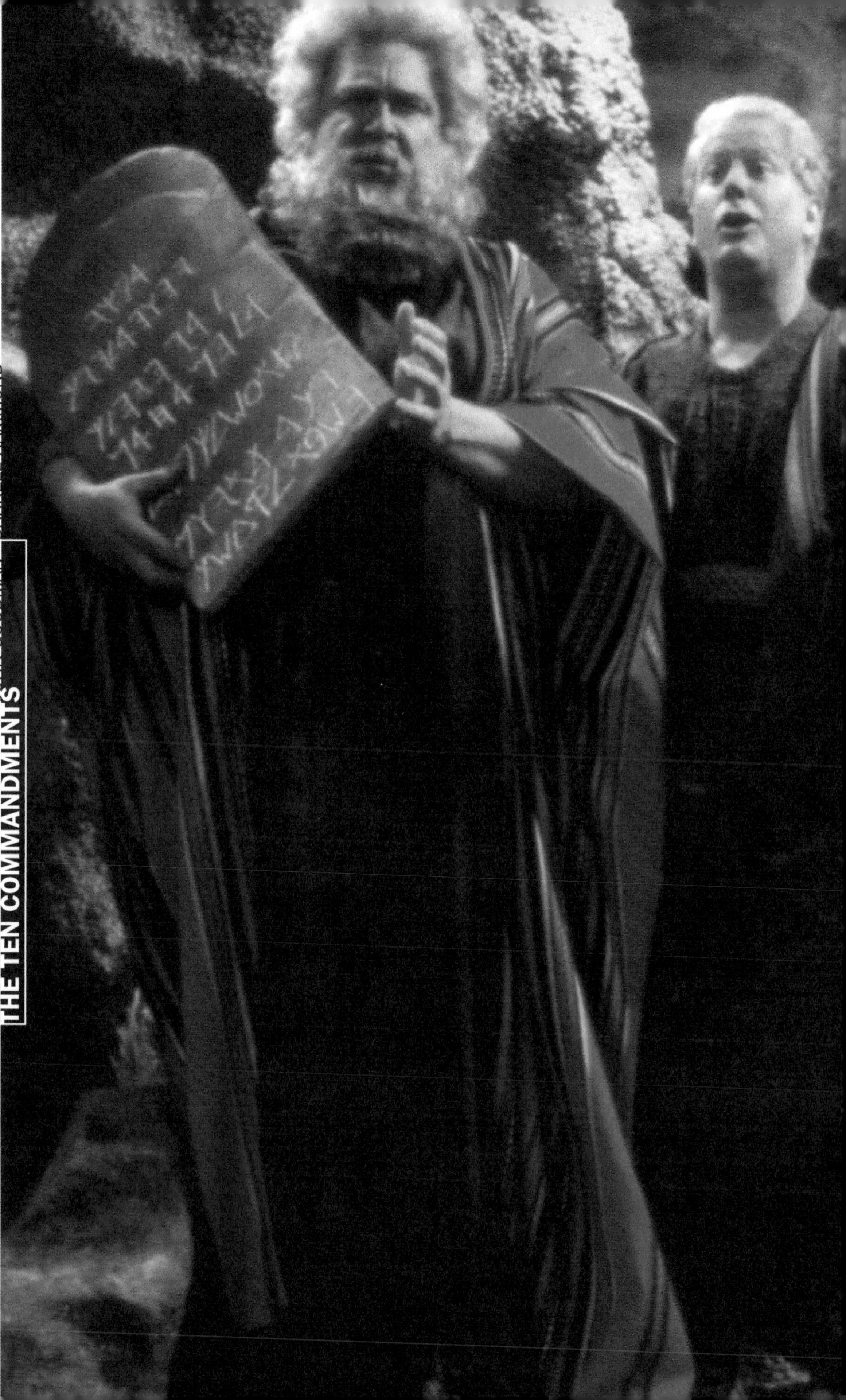

THE TEN COMMANDMENTS

JOHN GOODMAN DARRELL HAMMOND

Moses (BOOMING) :

. . . And the Lord has set before you this Fifth
Commandment, "Honor thy father and thy mother…"

Crowd: **Yes! It is good and just! Praise be!**

Moses: **And the Sixth Commandment, "Thou shalt not kill…"**

Crowd: **Yes! His will be done!**

Moses: **And the Seventh, "Thou shalt not commit adultery…"**

Crowd: **Hmmm. Adultery. I'm not so sure…**

Moses: **What? What did I say?**

Bill: **That last one is a little unclear…**

Moses: ## What? Someone dares question the word of God?!

CROWD PARTS AND AN ISRAELITE THAT LOOKS UNCANNILY LIKE BILL CLINTON, SPEAKS

Bill: **Well, no. Not question really. It's just a little unclear. I mean, "Adultery." What exactly does that mean, really?**

Moses: **Well, I think it's pretty self explanatory. Thou shalt not know any woman other than thy wife.**

Bill: **Yeah, right. But hear me out on this one. Is it technically adultery if, let's say, you just let a woman know you. You're not really knowing her back.**

Moses: **I don't follow.**

Bill: **Come on, Moses. You know. Maybe she knows you some other way…like not with her loins…she could even be fully dressed…**

Moses: ## Oh, come on! You're not asking what I think you're asking!

Bill: **What? You gotta admit it's really not that clear. Right, people?**

Crowd: **Well…**

Moses: **Yes, it is clear! What you're talking about is definitely adultery.**

Bill: **So, God told you that, exactly?**

Moses: **No, we didn't talk about that.**

Bill: **Well, then how do you know? This is pretty damn important. Maybe you should go ask Him.**

21

Linda TALKING INTO A HUGE FLOWER ON HER DRESS :

Monica Lewinsky!

Hiiiiiiii!

HUGS MONICA

Monica: **Ow.**

Linda: **You look nice.**

MONICA TAKES OFF HER COAT. HER DRESS HAS A LARGE STAIN ON IT.

Monica: **Thanks.**

It's my lucky dress.

23

Waiter:
What can I get you two ladies to drink?

Monica: **I'll have a Bardles And Jaimes**

I love B.J.'s.

Linda:

I'll have a Bloody Mary and two AA batteries.

A CNN / USA Today poll
says Americans believe
Hillary Rodham Clinton is

smarter than Bill

by a vote of forty percent
to twenty-two percent.

The President took it all
in stride, saying,

"No big deal.

It's only an eight percent
difference."

NORM MACDONALD

More O.J. Simpson news...

On Friday, **the Juice**

officially endorsed Bill Clinton
for President...

...adding, "I'd like to help him out

in any way

I can."

To which the President replied,

31

"Well,

there is one thing..."

Oh yeah, it's time for "The Ladies' Man."

Leon: **Welcome to "The Ladies' Man,"**
the love line with all the right responses
to your romantic queries.
I'm Leon Phelps and how y'all doing tonight?
I'm doin' fine, I got my Courvoisier here,
and very soon I will take your calls, but before I take any calls,
I will be joined tonight by a very sexy and special lady
who has done more to educate this country on the ways of love
than anyone else on the planet.

Would you please welcome my guest,

Miss Monica Lewinsky...

Yeah, well alright, you're looking good.

Monica: **Thank you, Leon.**

Leon: **Now, Miss Lewinsky will be quite helpful for us because I have been told that when it comes to matters of the heart, and her own personal relationships, she is known for showing very good judgment. Is that correct?**

Monica: **Yes, that's right, Leon.**

In fact, I'd say I've really only been wrong once.

Leon: **Well, we all make mistakes...that's why God invented the Mexican divorce.**

How about we take some callers?

Monica: **Okay!**

Leon: **Go ahead caller, you got the Ladies' Man...**

Caller 1: **Hello, Ladies' Man...**

Leon: **It's a lady. What seems to be your query?**

Caller 1: **I'm worried, you see, I've started a relationship with someone at work.**

Leon: **Yeah, well I know they always say that you should not dip your wang in the company ink,** but I think people should feel free to dip their wangs into anything around the office. White out, coffee, a box of paper clips—

Caller 1: **Anyway, this guy at work is considerably older than me... and also he's my boss.**

Leon: **Oh, your boss!**

Monica, maybe you should answer this one.

Monica: **Well, I would say it's not a good idea to get involved with people you work with. Believe me. First, people around the office start gossiping, and the next thing you know, your face is all over Arabic newspapers.**

Leon: **Yeah, the same thing is always happening to me.**

Go ahead, caller.

Caller 2: **Hello, Ladies' Man. My long time boyfriend recently took a job in another state, and this long distance relationship is tearing us apart.**

Do you think we should try phone sex?

Leon: **No, absolutely not. As one who's tried it, I can tell you It is not a good idea to have sex with a phone.**

Monica: **Leon, that isn't what phone sex is.**

Leon: **I know. But I had to try it anyway. I was drunk, and it was a Garfield phone, and I'll be damned if that little orange**

bastard didn't start to look real good one night. But anyway, Monica, maybe you can shed some light on this matter.

Monica: **Well...I did have phone sex with this one guy...**

his name doesn't matter.

Leon: **Why don't we just call him William Howard Taft. And I think you know who I mean by William Howard Taft.**

Monica: **Anyway, caller, my only advice about phone sex would be, if you do it...don't tell anybody about it...**

Leon: **Well you could probably tell your best friend, right?**

Monica: **No.**

Leon: **I mean if she were an older, unattractive-type lady?**

Monica: **Definitely not.**

Leon: **Okay, then. Next caller.**

Linda Tripp: **Hello, Ladies' Man.**

Leon: **Say, it's a...well, I'm not sure what it is..**

Linda Tripp: **It's Linda Tripp, Leon.**

Leon: **Well! It's Linda Tripp, everybody!** **Welcome to the show, Linda.**

Linda: **Thanks, Leon.** (HEAVY TRAFFIC ON A HIGHWAY)

Leon: **You have to speak up, Linda, I can barely hear you.**

Linda: **I am at a phone booth outside a Dunkin Donuts on the Jersey Turnpike. Traffic's pretty heavy.**

Leon: **What seems to be your query, Linda?**

Linda: **Well, you know how I'm the most hated person in America...**

Leon/Monica: **Yeah.**

37

Linda: **Well I was just wondering, since you have Monica on the show, maybe she could find it in her heart to forgive me.**
Monica: **Forgive you? After what —**

wait, what's that clicking noise, Linda?

Are you recording this?

Linda: No, people driving by are throwing cans and bottles at me... so, what do you say, Monica, do you think you could forgive me?

Monica: # No way!

Leon: Well, there you have it. You heard it here first. For the rest of her life, Miss Lewinsky will hold a bitter, heartfelt, grudge against John Goodman... That's about all the time we have on "The Ladies' Man." But before I go, I'd be remiss if I didn't ask you the one question that's on everyone's mind...

Monica: Okay...

Leon: Just exactly how big... do you think the opening weekend for "Star Wars" will be?

Monica: Oh, it'll be huge.

Leon: I knew it! Thanks, Monica. And we'll see you next time on

"The Ladies' Man."

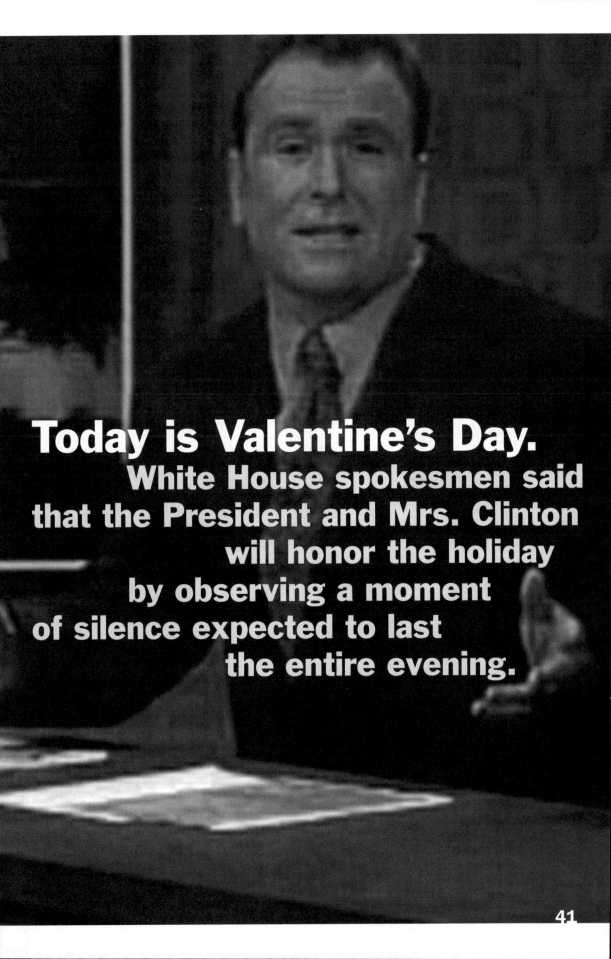

Today is Valentine's Day.
White House spokesmen said
that the President and Mrs. Clinton
will honor the holiday
by observing a moment
of silence expected to last
the entire evening.

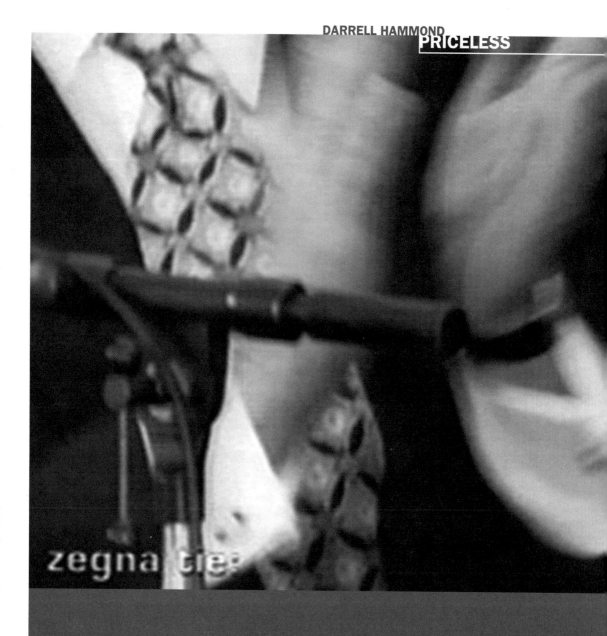

zegna tie:

One Davidoff cigar. Seven dollars.

cigar:

One Zegna tie. One hundred and ten dollars.

One Gap cotton dress.
Thirty-four dollars.

gap cotton dress:

Making Yasir Arafat wait
     while you and a friend masturbate...

Priceless.

There are some things money can't buy.

for everything else th

For everything else, there's Mastercard.
Accepted all over...
...Even in our highest office.

e's MasterCa

This week, veteran news anchorman
David Brinkley apologized to Bill
Clinton for an election night commentary
in which he called
the President "boring
and uncreative."

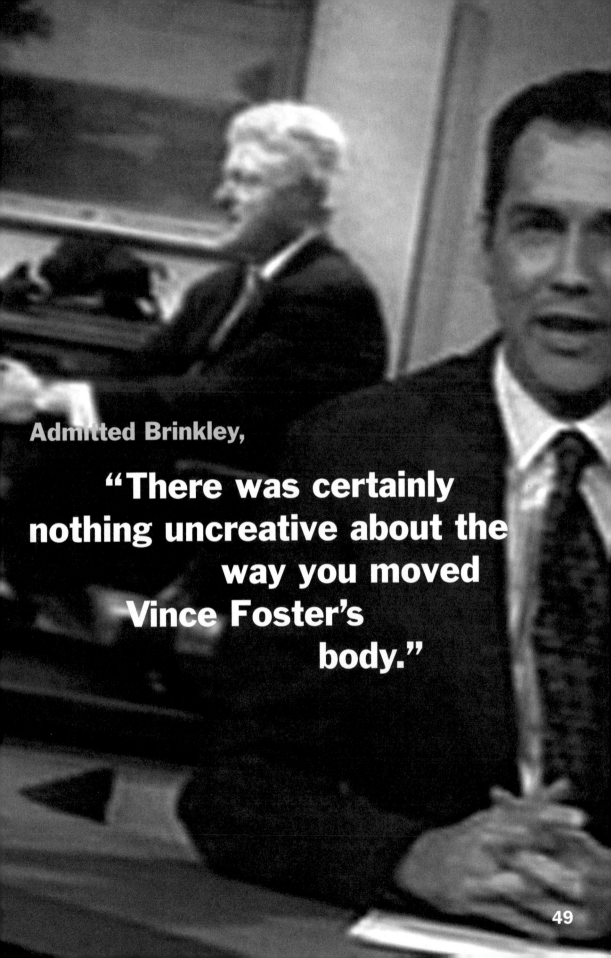

Admitted Brinkley,

"There was certainly nothing uncreative about the way you moved Vince Foster's body."

Thelma: **Hello, and welcome to "The Oprah Show," for**
January 11th, 2002.
WAVES PORKCHOP

Mmmm this porkchop is good, baby!...And now, here's Oprah!

Oprah: **Thank you, Thelma. That, of course, my sidekick for the past three years, Thelma Weston! Hello, everybody, and welcome to "Oprah"! Boy, honey, I can't believe 2001 is already over, can you?**

AUDIENCE APPLAUSE

Oprah: **Well, we've got some show for you today.**

Remember this from a few years ago? READING FROM AN INDEX CARD

"I did not have improper relations with that woman."

AUDIENCE LAUGHS NOSTALGICALLY

That's right! It's been almost four years, but we've got the gang from the Monica Lewinsky scandal here with us today! AUDIENCE APPLAUSE

Let's bring 'em out!

You know him as the former President of the United States... **William Jefferson Clinton!**

DARRELL COMES ON AS CLINTON WITH AN OPEN SHIRT AND MUSTACHE. HE IS A LITTLE TOO TAN. HE GIVES A BIG WAVE.

Clinton: **Oprah, good to see you, baby.**

BILL KISSES OPRAH, SITS.

Oprah: **And here's Bill's ex-wife. Let's hear it for my girl, the former First Lady, Hillary Rodham!**

HILLARY JOGS OUT, WAVES. SHE IS DRESSED VERY EARTHY, LOTS OF SILVER AND JADE AND A BILLOWY LINEN DRESS. SHE KISSES OPRAH.

Hillary TO BILL: **Hey, you!** THEY HIGH-FIVE AND SHE SITS.

Oprah: **And what would the Clinton scandal be without...Monica Lewinsky!**

MONICA COMES ON, SHE KISSES OPRAH, SMILES, GIVES BILL AND HILLARY A LITTLE WAVE, SITS.

Oprah: **This guy was always my favorite...Independent Counsel,**
Kenneth Starr!

PARNELL COMES ON AS STARR IN A JOGGING SUIT, GIVING A BIG "WHO ME?" LOOK. LAUGHS, WAVES, SITS.

Oprah: **And finally the woman without whom none of these people**
would be here today... **Linda Tripp!**

JOHN GOODMAN COMES ON AS LINDA TRIPP, LAUGHING. THEY HUG, HE SITS.

Oprah: **Alright, everybody! Now four years ago,**
you guys were involved in a big, big scandal —

Bill: **Who me?** THEY ALL LAUGH.

Oprah: **Yes you, Bill. Now, looking back, do you have any regrets?**

Clinton: **I do, Oprah. I just wish at the time that I**
had gotten to know Ken a little sooner.

Linda: **I have one regret, Oprah.** LINDA CHOKES UP.

Oprah: **Linda, do you have something you want to say to Monica?**

Linda: **Yes, Oprah. Monica, I want to say**

I am so sorry...that I said
you looked fat in that blue dress.

Monica: **Linda, that is so sweet!...**
You're not recording this, are you?

THEY ALL LAUGH

Oprah: **It's so great to see you guys laughing like this!**
Do you get together? Do you socialize?

Bill: **Well it's so hard.**

I'm in L.A. working with Dreamworks, Hillary's in Santa Fe —

Hillary: **Doing my pottery thing.**

Bill: **And then we were all gonna get together in Aspen last winter, but Linda couldn't make it.**

Linda: **I had some outpatient surgery, unfortunately.**

Monica: **How are the feet?**

Linda: **The feet are good. The feet are good.**

Oprah: **And Kenneth, you're not in D.C. anymore, either?**

Kenneth: **No, actually I'm in Toronto now. And I just couldn't be happier. I've realized that everything I did back then wasn't about the Clintons or "obstruction of justice." I was in a bad marriage and... just not in a healthy place.**

Oprah: **But now you're re-married.**

Kenneth: **Well, no, I'm living with someone now.**

Connie. She's a physical therapist.

(WAVING) # Hey, baby!

53

Oprah: **Bill, what was the moment when you knew things were out of control?**
Bill: **Mmm. I remember one night in the Oval Office,**
I was on the phone with Madeline Albright, eating pizza,
chomping on a cigar,

coked out of my mind —

Monica: (LAUGHING) # I remember that night!

Bill: **And I just thought...I'm the President of the United States, this is nuts.**

I'm gonna end up like Tupac.

Oprah: **But you didn't stop there, did you?**
Bill: **No, I did not.**
Oprah: **Because you got in trouble again after the Lewinsky scandal.**

You had another affair...in the Spring of 1999, with a paralegal
who was working on your civil suit,
Tina Baxter.

Bill: **I mean, what can I say? I got the touch!** DARRELL DOES CLINTON THUMB & LIP.
Oprah: **Well let's bring her out! Surprise! Tina Baxter!**
Bill: (LAUGHING) **You're kiddin' me!**

CAMERON COMES OUT AS A WELL-DRESSED YOUNG WOMAN.
EVERYONE STANDS AND GREETS HER, SHE SITS, HOLDS HANDS WITH WHOEVER'S NEARBY.

Live from New York,

Tina: **Oprah, I have to tell you how lucky I feel to have been a part of this scandal.** I mean, these people did so much work!

Oprah: **You are all so great together, I just wanna know, is there any chance you might team up again and give us a new scandal?**

Linda: **Well, we're not allowed to say anything for sure, but we've been talking —**
Monica: **It's definitely a possibility.**

Oprah: **Well, you've given us so much, already. Thank you for making history.** The cast of the Clinton/Lewinsky scandal everyone! Let's hear it!

AUDIENCE STANDS AND APPLAUDS. CAST GETS UP AND HUGS TEARFULLY.
Oprah: **We'll be back with more of this crazy gang...plus,**

it's Saturday Night!!!

Rejecting conspiracy theories that President Clinton killed Vince Foster, a report out this week from Independent Counsel Kenneth Starr has officially concluded that Foster took his own life. Among other things, the report cites evidence that Foster was deeply depressed in the days leading up to his death.

Although, the report

le Confirm

concedes Foster was depressed because President Clinton was trying to murder him.

COLIN QUINN

Okay, we've been off for two weeks, so we've had plenty
of time to think about this Clinton thing,
and I really feel bad for him.

I mean, this man is so full
of self-hatred that he puts a
lifetime of achievement on
the line for a series of
Olive Garden hostesses.

You know why Clinton denied being with Monica Lewinsky? Because she's not that hot. Most guys have done this, made it with the ugly girl at the bar, and the next day your friends are ribbing you.

"You did her last night."

"No, I didn't."

"Yeah, you

You swear you didn't.

did.”

Then she comes into the bar all dolled up because she thinks she has a boyfriend.

She's got a new hat.

You have to stop her.

She starts hugging you.

You saw how Clinton hugged her.

It was that "morning after" hug.

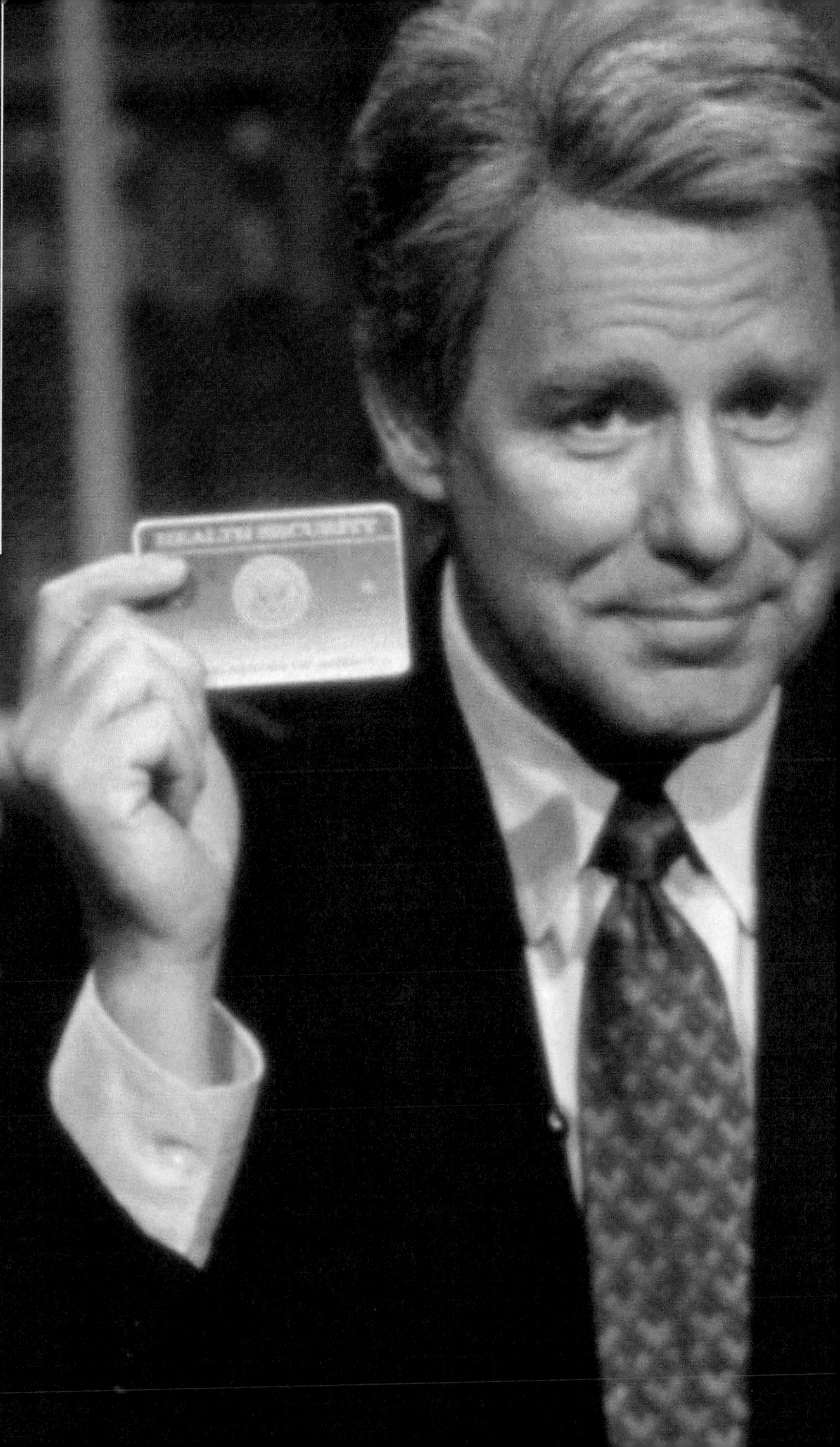

PHIL HARTMAN
CLINTON HEALTH PLAN COLD OPEN

Bill: Good evening. This past Wednesday night I laid out the basics of a health care plan that would guarantee every American a comprehensive package of medical coverage. If you are a citizen of the United States, YOU CANNOT BE TURNED DOWN! That's right! If you have an obstructed calcified pancreas, you qualify. If you have a prolapsed colon, you qualify.

If you need a sebaceous cyst lanced and drained, you qualify! You see, over the last eight months Hillary and I visited with thousands of troubled Americans who shared their anxieties with us. I remember the anguish of a man in Virginia who told me he lives with the constant worry that if a loved one were to cut off his penis again, he could not afford to have it reattached. That he would be forced to keep it in the refrigerator until he found a new job with the proper coverage. Hillary has heard from countless others who go to sleep every night fearing that the next time they drink a Pepsi they will swallow a syringe. I've visited sideshows throughout our great nation. And for the first time, under our plan, the World's Thinnest Man, you are covered. Japu, the India Rubber Man, you are covered. Lobster Boy, I feel your pain. You are covered! But you, "The Boy Who Was Raised By Wolves," are not covered because you are a fraud. It's just a wig. And I bring up Wolf Boy for a reason. We simply must draw the line somewhere. We cannot pay for everything.

For example, cooties are covered. But not the heebee jeebees.

Cabin fever — covered. Lotto fever — not covered.
Fumblitis, covered,
but butterfingers, not covered.
Breast augmentation...

(THINKS ABOUT IT)

...covered.

Breast reduction, not covered.

A frightening moment this week for First Lady Hillary Clinton. Her plane, en route to the former Soviet Union, was forced to make an emergency landing when it was discovered that a frayed wire in the engine was causing serious malfunctions.

The President was said to be furious, and demanded an immediate investigation of what went wrong with

"Operation Frayed Wire."

CNN and
P

THE H

O

PRESID

SCA

Kraft Foods
sent

STORY

F

ENTIAL

NDAL

In an attempt to put the current White House Scandal
in perspective, CNN and Kraft Foods
have joined together to present
"The History
of Presidential Scandals."

Most of us now know that Franklin Roosevelt had
a longtime extramarital affair with Lucy Mercer.

And that Thomas Jefferson
fathered illegitimate children
by Sally Hemings, one of
his slaves.

But few people know that in the spring of 1867, Andrew
Johnson had sex with a bird. Johnson's affair with the
sparrow was no secret among the Washington elite, and
is even alluded to in political cartoons of the time.

SEX NOT THE BIRD

This may be how Johnson earned the nickname, The Carolina Birdbagger.

L.B.J. was known to his Mexican whores as El B.J.

NORM MACDONALD

This week, President Clinton made history when he nominated

Madeline Albright

to be the first female Secretary of State. Responding to critics who says she's not the best choice, the President insisted,

"She looks a lot better after a couple of drinks."

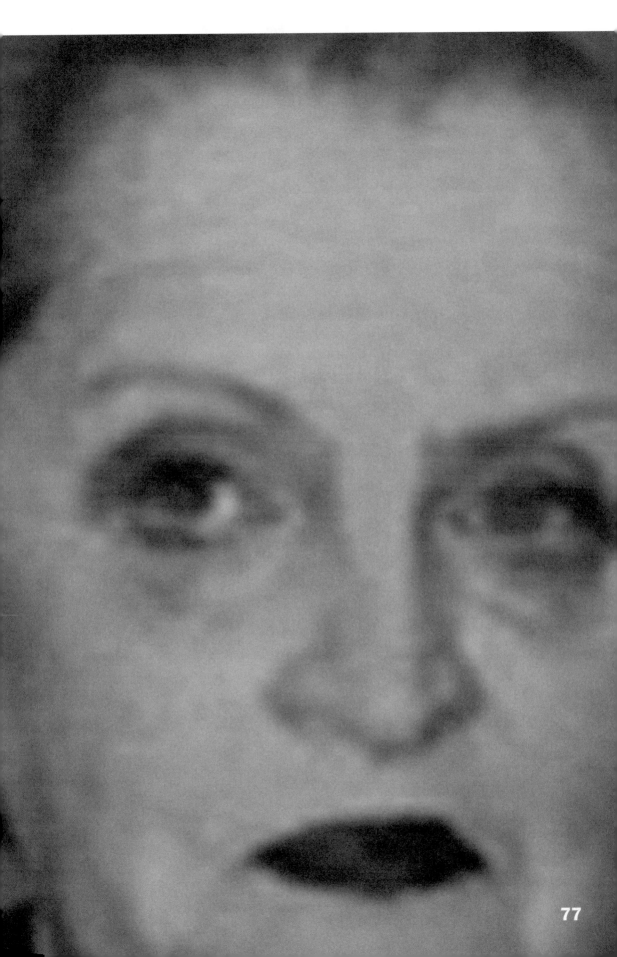

Good evening. For the past two weeks, our nation, along with our NATO allies, have been involved in an effort to halt Serbian aggression in the former Yugoslav province of Kosovo. Very early on, I was honest and forthright in saying that we would not use ground troops, under any circumstance. I was telling the truth. What a stupid idea.

The first time I tell the truth during my six years in office and it screws everything up.

Anyway, after reviewing the facts, and considering my spiritual advisors, I've determined that

honesty...is... a bad policy.

(THUMB, BITE LIP)

I'm going back to my old style. So everybody listen up.

I will **NOT** send ground troops into that country, Kosovo. Remember that. Well listen up, Serbia, I did not give orders to have Milosevic assassinated. I do not want his head on a stick.

And after he is gone, I have no intention of throwing a kick-ass all-night keg party in the Lincoln Bedroom. And late at that party, I will not go up to Kate, the new girl we hired, and I will not be wearing a fake mustache, and I will not say, **"The President's gone, my name's Mack, do you want to fool around?"**

This week in South Africa,

Winnie Mandela

was removed from the new government by her
husband, President Nelson Mandela.

A curious Bill Clinton

later called Mr. Mandela to find out

how exactly you go about
doing something like that.

...The Republicans screwed up... they pushed the impeachment thing too far...they ignored the polls, they underestimated the minority voters. **I haven't seen anybody misread a room this badly since Bill Clinton whipped it out in front of Paula Jones.** Meanwhile, on the news, the graphics still say "White House in Crisis"... they should be saying, **"White House Laughing Their Asses Off."**

Clinton's gone from
"Slick Willie" to
"I'm **rubber,** you're **glue,**
whatever you say
bounces off me
and **sticks** onto **you."**

They finally realized this thing has been dragging on too long, so now Clinton only has one final hurdle: **Henry Hyde's eighty-one questions.**

(TAKES OUT PROP SCRIPT)

Like question forty-one, which is a thirteen-parter which says, "As to each, do you admit or deny that you gave the following **gifts to Monica Lewinsky** at any time in the past:

A pin of the New York skyline..."

Is this guy a hillbilly or what? "...A large Rockettes blanket..."

Another airport gift. "...An Annie Lennox CD..." That must have been like, "Oh, Bill, you're so with it!" "... A box of cherry chocolates..."

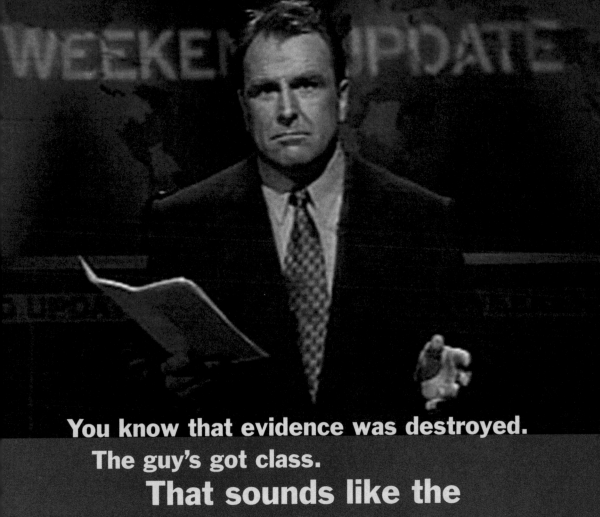

You know that evidence was destroyed.
The guy's got class.
That sounds like the
gift pack they give you
after you appear on the
"Jerry Springer Show."

UPDATE: PAULA JONES

Clinton sat across from Paula Jones today as he gave his deposition in her sexual harassment lawsuit. As he looked at her, he said,

"I never exposed myself to this woman. The woman I exposed myself to was a skank with a bad perm."

WILL FERRELL MOLLY SHANNON CHERI OTERI ANA GASTEYER JIMMY FALLON CHRIS KATTAN
IMPEACHMENT HEARINGS COLD OPEN

WILL FERRELL AS HENRY HYDE

Henry : . . . Alright. The committee will now turn its attention to the very grave and serious act of oral sex. To learn more about this topic we have invited several distinguished experts. Please state your names.

Courtney: **Courtney Love.**

Henry: **Ms. Love, the wisdom and experience you bring to this committee, in all matters of oral sex with numerous partners, honors the committee, and we thank you for your brave testimony.**

Courtney: **Thank you, Chairman Hyde.**

Henry: **Additional witnesses, state your names.**

CHERI AS MARIAH CAREY

Mariah: **Mariah Carey.**

ANA AS ELIZABETH DOLE

Elizabeth: **Elizabeth Dole.**

Henry: **Liddy, it's especially great to see you.**

Elizabeth:
Well, thank you, Henry. But I must say I'm not sure why I'm here. I am truly honored to be before this committee. I wouldn't say I'm an expert on this subject, but I'm happy to share with you the little that I know, if it helps the investigation.
Henry: **Well, Liddy, you'd make a formidable Presidential candidate. Additional witnesses.**

JIMMY, AS RICHARD SIMMONS

Richard: **Richard Simmons.**

KATTAN, AS GEORGE MICHAEL

George: **George Michael.**
Henry: **Welcome all. Now Ms. Love, how many times have you committed the act of oral sex?**
Courtney: **Twenty-one thousand, three hundred eighty-seven and a half.**

Henry: **Mr. Michael?**

George:

Is that Pre-Wham or Post-Wham?

Oprah: **So what's the book called?**

Monica: **It's called, "How To Give The President a Hummer." I wanted to call it, "How To Make Mouth Love To A President," but I just invented that phrase this morning.**

Oprah: **Child, you just told me you didn't have oral sex with the President!**

HOW TO GIVE THE PRESIDENT A HUMMER

by Monica Lewinsky

Monica:

I didn't!

The title is just to get people to buy the book.

OPRAH IS TAKEN ABACK AS SHE LOOKS INSIDE OF THE BOOK

Oprah: **Then why's there a picture of you giving oral sex to the President?**

Monica: **Alright, Oprah, you got me. But I only did it that one time, to take the picture for the book.**

In a "Playboy" interview, Pamela Anderson, who left her husband after he beat her, says that she cannot understand why Hillary Clinton is sticking with her husband after all he's done.

Because he is the most powerful man in the world—not a drummer for an '80s' hair band.

The White House

says that surviving relatives of those who died in a forty-year-old federal study which allowed men infected with syphilis to go untreated will get an official apology from President Clinton. According to the President,

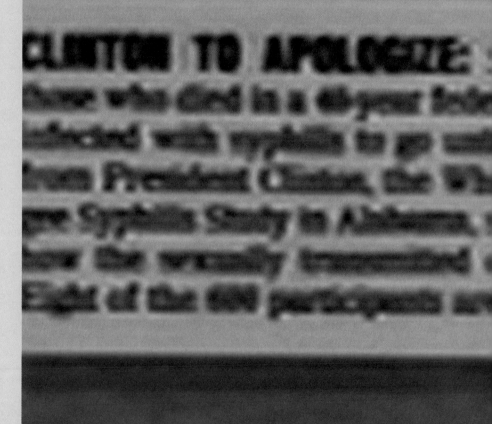

"If not for the sacrifices made by these brave men, I would not be alive today."

President Clinton told junior high school students in Washington this week that sex is not a sport, but a

"responsibility."

And according to Arkansas State Troopers, he used to be responsible four or five nights a week.

NORM MACDONALD

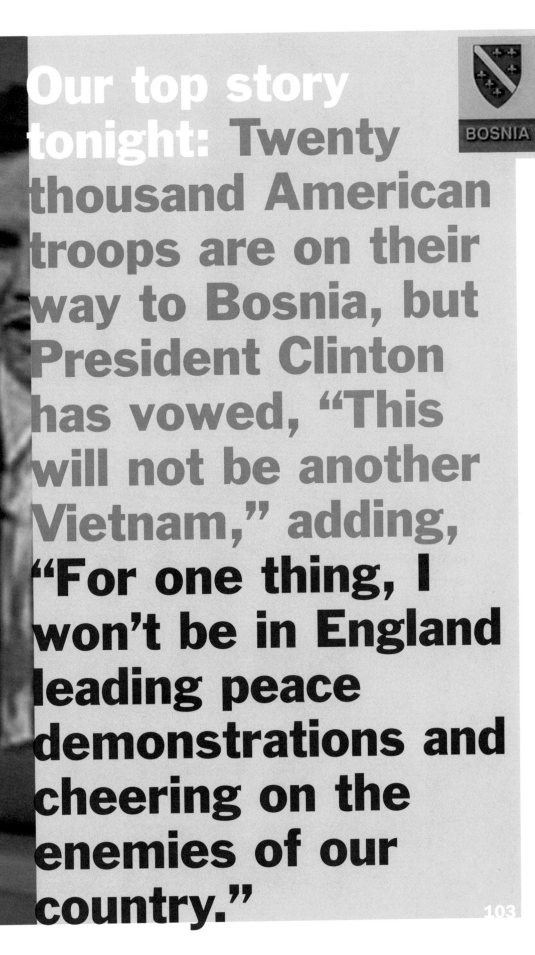

Our top story tonight: Twenty thousand American troops are on their way to Bosnia, but President Clinton has vowed, "This will not be another Vietnam," adding, "For one thing, I won't be in England leading peace demonstrations and cheering on the enemies of our country."

BOSNIA

103

Gramm

He'd B

WASHIN

ters) — Sen

as, who is

can Preside

Declares

est Clinton

Republican Presidential candidate Phil Gramm of Texas said yesterday that if he and President Clinton met in the general election next year, he would, quote,

"Chew him up and spit him out."

President Clinton, on the other hand, says he would take Gramm,

deep fry him, dip him in mayonnaise and swallow him whole.

Despite pressure,

Jim and Susan MacDougal, jailed Whitewater swindlers, are still refusing to testify about President Clinton's role in the scandal, and some are charging that the President has secretly promised them a pardon in return for their silence. Well, in a candid interview this week, the President admitted he might consider pardoning the two, but only after making "every effort"

to have them killed in prison.

COLIN QUINN

Last weekend,
President Clinton and
the First Lady went
to Stanford University
to meet Chelsea's
new boyfriend,

Matthew Pierce.

Pierce told Clinton
that the President
was "his role model,"
to which Clinton
responded,

First Folks check out Chelsea's new beau

"I don't want you seeing my daughter anymore."

Saddam (ANSWERS PHONE): **Chillo, you got Saddam.**
Bill: **Saddam? It me, Bill Clinton.**

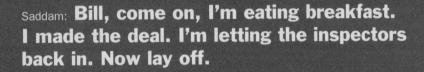

Saddam: **Bill, come on, I'm eating breakfast. I made the deal. I'm letting the inspectors back in. Now lay off.**

Bill: **Well, that's what I'm calling you about. You see, I was thinking maybe you could NOT let the inspectors in. What do you think?**
Saddam: **Have you been drinking, Bill?**
Bill: **No! Yes, but look, buddy, I need you to help me out here. This Monica Lewinsky thing is getting pretty hot again. I could use a distraction.**
Saddam: **Like the Mamet movie, "Wag the Dog"?**
Bill: **Mamet?**
Saddam: **With that lesbian girl and DeNiro and Dustin. I thought Dustin was fabulous! You know, he may be hell on the set, but he's heaven on the screen.**
Bill: **Look, Sadbuddy, you're getting off the subject . . . Couldn't you spray a few kurds with Anthrax?**

Saddam: **Come on, Bill. Anthrax is horrible, it makes me sick.**
Bill: **Well I need something. I've got to get this sex stuff out of the headlines.**
(CALL WAITING BEEP)
Bill: **Hold on a second, I got another call coming in . . .**
(CLICK)
Bill: **Hello?**
SPLIT SCREEN: DARRELL AND MOLLY, AS MONICA LEWINSKY. SHE ALSO IS IN BED, TALKING ON A PRINCESS TEEN PHONE. A TV FLICKER ILLUMINATES THE ROOM)

Monica: **Hey.**

Bill: **Hey, Monica! I was just going to call you!**

Monica: **Oh, my God. It's like we have the same brain. I miss you! What are you doing?**

Bill: **I got Saddam on the other line. Looks like there ain't gonna be a war...**

Monica: **Well that bites.**

Bill: **Anyway, how's that Starr thing going?**

Monica: **I don't know . . . and anyway, it's totally dumb. Are you watching "Dawson's Creek"?**

Bill: **No, I'm taping it, and DON'T tell me what happens to Pacey.**

Monica: **Okay. Let me say hi to Saddam.**

Bill: **Hold on one second...**

(CLICK) (CUT TO; DARRELL ALONE)

Bill: **Saddam, you still there?**

(3-WAY SPLIT SCREEN: DARRELL, MOLLY AND WILL)

Saddam: **Who was that, one of your Jewish friends?**

Bill: **No! Well yes, sort of...**

Monica: **Hey, Saddam!**

Saddam: **Monica! You never call me anymore! Thanks for the beret. I love it!**

Monica: **You're so cute! Bill won't wear his.**

UPDATE: CLINTON COMMUNION

While visiting an African Catholic
Church, President Clinton, a Baptist,
received communion.

Luckily,

his advisors stopped him from entering a confessional after they calculated that his penance would be six million Our Fathers and eighteen million Hail Marys.

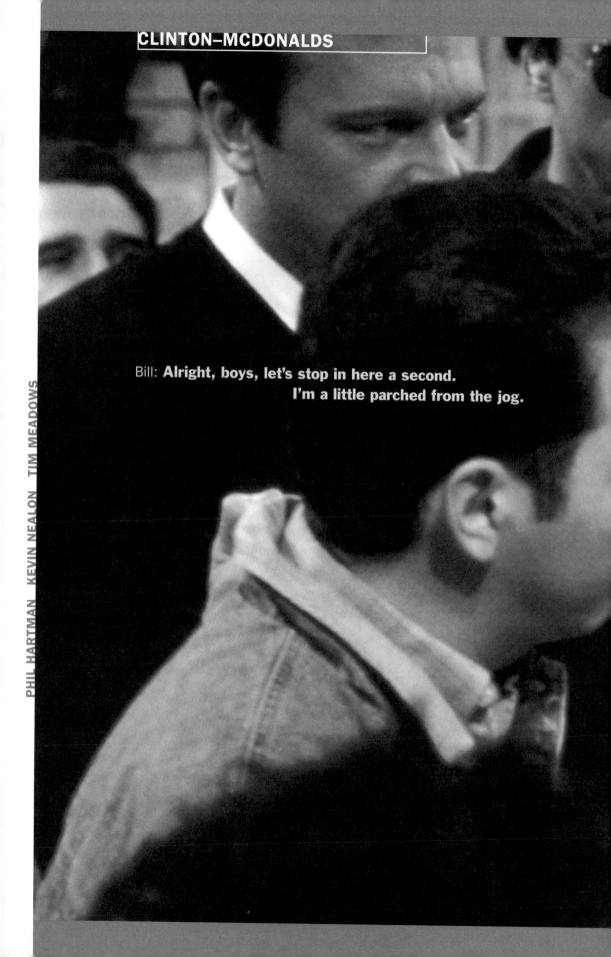

Bill: **Alright, boys, let's stop in here a second.**
I'm a little parched from the jog.

Secret Service Agent: **Sir, we've only been jogging for three blocks. Besides, Mrs. Clinton asked us not to let you in any more fast food places.**

Bill: **I just want to mingle with the American people, talk with some real folks, and maybe get a diet Coke . . . or somethin.'**

Secret Service Agent: **Fine. But please don't tell Mrs. Clinton.**

Bill:

**Jim, let me tell you something.
There's gonna be
a bunch a things
we don't tell Mrs.
Clinton about.**

This week, President Clinton told an audience of high school students that Bosnia won't become his Vietnam.
The President said his plan is to drag his heels long enough that Bosnia becomes

Al Gore's Vietnam.

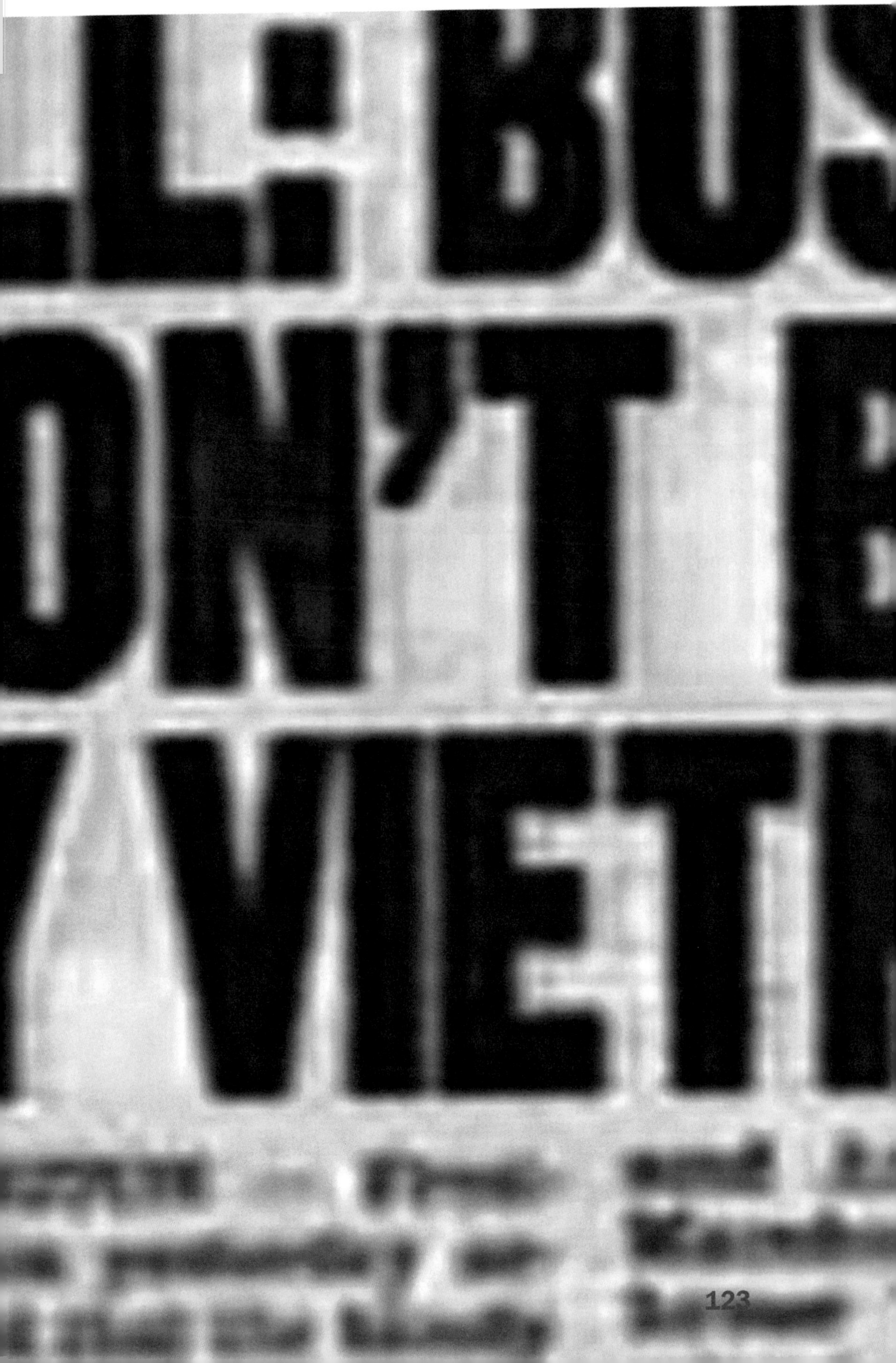
LL: BUS
ON'T B
VIET

LIVE

Todd: **Welcome back to E! Entertainment television. We're broadcasting live this morning from Washington, D.C., from one of the sexiest, hottest events in the country, the Impeachment Trial of William Jefferson Clinton. I'm Todd Newton.**

Melissa: **And I'm Melissa Rivers.**

ENTERTAINMENT TELEVISION

JIMMY FALLON   CHERI OTERI   WILL FERRELL   DARRELL HAMMOND   GWYNETH PALTROW

Todd: **This has been so cool. We've been camped out here since four o'clock this morning to talk to all the stars of the trial as they make their way down the red carpet.**

Melissa: **And Todd, I've been pretty cold out here in just my Pamela Dennis gown and this Harry Winston choker. Borrowed, of course.**

Todd: **Ha ha ha ha ha ha ha ha ha ha ha ha ha. Awesome. Wow. Here comes Chief Justice William Rehnquist.**

Melissa/Todd: **Bill! Bill! Over here! Come talk to E!**

(WILL ENTERS AS REHNQUIST IN HIS IMPEACHMENT ROBE)

William: **Good morning.**

Todd: **Bill's the Chief Justice of the Supreme Court. He's presiding over the impeachment trial.**

Melissa: **But you might also know him from Abortion. Bill, you look amazing. Who are you wearing?**

William: **Actually, I designed this myself. I copied it from a Gilbert & Sullivan operetta I saw.**

Melissa: **Turn around. Can you see this?** (WILL DOES A PROUD TWIRL) **Do you like dressing up for these things?**

William: **I do. I think people expect a little glamour. And I'm happy to —**

Melissa: **Oh my God! There's Trent Lott.** (WILL IS BRUSHED ASIDE)

Melissa/Todd: **Trent! Trent! Over here! It's E!**

(DARRELL ENTERS AS TRENT LOTT)

Trent: **Hi. How's it going?**

Todd: **Wow. Trent Lott, I just have to say, you are even more awesome in person than you are on C-Span. I love you. I think you're the bomb.**

Trent: **Thank you, young man.**

Melissa: **Now Trent, you are the Governor of Missouri.**

Trent: **Senator from Mississippi.**

Melissa: **And you are a Republican. Do you think you're gonna win today?**

Trent: **Well, it's not about winning. I'm just happy to be impeaching the President.**

RICH FRANCESE   CHRIS PARNELL   TIM MEADOWS   CHRIS KATTAN

William Rehnquist

Trent Lott

Todd: **You are such a gentleman. Such a class act. I love you. I'm in love with you. I want to make love on you.**

Trent: **Okay, gotta go. You all have a pleasant morning.**

Todd: **I am totally star-struck right now. I can't believe I just met Trent Lott.**

Melissa: **I did not like his hair.**

(GWYNETH ENTERS AS SHARON STONE WITH RICH FRANCESE AS HER CREEPY "SAN FRANCISCO EXAMINER" HUSBAND)

Melissa: **And here's Sharon Stone. Sharon, who are you wearing?**

Sharon: **This was made for me by my friend, Vera Wang. Don't you love it?**

Melissa **I love you, Sharon. Now, are you testifying today or are you presenting...?**

Sharon: **I'm just here to promote my new movie "Gloria."** (APPLAUDS HERSELF) **And I'm not going home until I meet Charles Ruff, because I think people in wheelchairs are the real heroes!**

Melissa: **Is this your husband?**

Sharon: **Yes, isn't he creepy?**

Todd: **Here comes Bob Barr! He's one of the House Managers.** (JIMMY DRAGS PARNELL ON AS BOB BARR) **Don't you try to sneak by!**

Bob: **Hey, I wouldn't do that to you, Todd.**

Sharon: **Bob! Kiss kiss!**

Todd: **Bob, the Senate has set a deadline of February 12th to end this trial. But we've got to ask you —**

Melissa: **What did you think of "Patch Adams"?**

Bob: **I loved it. It's a modern parable. And, you know, with Robin Williams, you always get something new and different. That guy's great.**

Melissa: **Who are you wearing?**

Bob: **The suit is Today's Man and the shirt is a short sleeve button down, I don't know if you can see this, by Structure. It's a medium.**

Todd: **Um, Sharon, you can go inside now if you want.**

Sharon: (SMILING VACANTLY AT CAMERA) **Actually, I'd prefer to stay on camera, Todd.**

Todd: **Well, okay. Here comes the couple of the hour! It's Betty Currie and Andy Dick!**

(KATTAN AND TIM ENTER AS ANDY DICK AND BETTY CURRIE)

Betty: **What's up, freaks? Are you ready to party?**

Andy: **Oh my God, Todd Newton. I would make out with you if we were girls! What am I saying?**

Melissa: **You and Betty seem so in love.**

Todd: **You guys look awesome together. Do I hear wedding bells?**

Melissa: **I just got married. Look at my ring!** (CHERI HOLDS UP A RING THE SIZE OF A DOORKNOB)

Andy: **Oh my God. I'd buy a ring like that for Betty if I weren't so coked up and gay. What? Why am I talking?**

Melissa: (LAUGHS) **Don't go away, everybody. E! will be right back.**

Sharon Stone

Rep. Bob Barr

Andy Dick
Betty Currie

127

Todd:

We're live at the impeachment of the President with Bob Barr, Sharon Stone, Betty Currie, Andy Dick, Joan Rivers's daughter and —

Hey! I think this might be the Apocalypse.

This is exactly what St. John predicted. Yup, here comes

a wall of fire and —

Melissa: **Mom!**

Norm: **"An American President," Rob Reiner's new film starring Michael Douglas and Annette Bening, opened in theaters last week.**

Here with his review is Update movie critic and Forty-Second President of the United States, Bill Clinton.

Bill: **Thank you, Norm. Rob Reiner's latest film tells the story of a young, idealistic President who not only has a hostile Congress and a nasty Republican challenger to contend with, but has to raise a twelve-year-old daughter on his own because, you see, his wife is dead.**

I loved this movie.

Norm: **Wow, you really liked it that much, Mr. President?**

Bill: **Norm, from the moment we learn the premise about the young President and the dead wife, the viewer just falls hook, line and sinker. I mean, Rob Reiner has tapped into what must be every young American's fantasy. To grow up, be President, have your wife die, and be left with all the trappings of the office, free and unattached.**

Norm: **Was there anything you didn't like about the movie, Mr. President?**

Bill: **I thought some of the performances were unconvincing, particularly Martin Sheen as the President's Chief of Staff. He's done better work.**

Norm: **What did you like best about the movie?**

Bill: # The dead wife.

Norm: **Now, Mr. President, one thing that I wondered about in the movie; would it really be possible for a President to sneak a woman into the White House with all the staff, and all the security, and not have one of them talk to the press?**

Bill: **Why? What did you hear?**

Norm: **Nothing, I didn't hear anything, but with that huge White House staff, surely one of them would talk to the press.**

Bill: **No, seriously, did you hear anything?**

Norm: **No, no, I didn't hear anything.**

Bill: **Oh, good.**

Norm: **So anyway, on a scale of one to ten, what did you give this film?**

Bill: **Norm,** TURNS TO CAMERA

I give it a ten!

Norm: **Ten? Wow, that's more than you gave "Tank Girl."**

Bill: **I loved this movie.**

Norm: **President Bill Clinton, everybody...**

135

CLINTON GLOATING COLD OPEN

Bill: **There is also a concern that I, and all my White House colleagues, will gloat.**
Let me assure you, and our distinguished Senators, that as I successfully finish my term in office and complete one of the most prosperous periods in our history, **I WILL NOT GLOAT.**

Let me assure you...

TIM, AS VERNON JORDAN, ENTERS AND STANDS BEHIND DARRELL

**...that my vindicated friend,
Vernon Jordan, WILL NOT GLOAT.**

TIM SHAKES HIS HEAD MEANINGFULLY, BRIEFLY FIGHTING A SMILE

Let me also assure you that my wife, Hillary,

ANA ENTERS AS HILLARY AND STANDS BEHIND DARRELL

**the next Senator from New York State,
WILL ALSO NOT GLOAT. Neither will
my Vice President, Al Gore,**

WILL ENTERS AS AL GORE AND STANDS BEHIND DARRELL.
ALL FIGHT SMILES AND GIGGLES

who waits quietly to decimate George Bush's little son. Al Gore **WILL NOT GLOAT.** And finally, rest assured that Monica Lewinsky,

MOLLY ENTERS AS MONICA LEWINSKY AND STANDS BEHIND DARRELL

my once and future girlfriend, **WILL ALSO NOT GLOAT.**

I mean, why should we? Why should I gloat? I've been IMPEACHED.

By the HOUSE OF REPRESENTATIVES.

Think about it.

That's a whole big **HOUSE.** Filled with all kinds of important **REPRESENTATIVES.**

OTHERS OCCASIONALLY FIGHT BACK SMILES AND GIGGLES.

137

Bill: **Larry, you've been a big help. You ratting out Bob Starr for his sexual indiscretions has taken some of the heat off me.**

Larry Flynt: **I'm just giving the Republicans a taste of their own medicine.**

Bill: **How do you find them?**

Larry: **I hire investigators to follow the congressman and when —**

Bill: **No, not that. Those women that pose nude in your** magazine. **Where do you get 'em? I do alright, but none of them will let me take pictures of 'em.**

Receptionist: **Mr. President, your wife is here.**   Bill: **Party's over.**

Hillary: **What are you doing in here with that whoremonger?**

Bill: **Are you talking to him or me?**

Reporter:

Linda, you are the **most hated person in America.**

Linda: **I'm not sure that's true.**

Reporter: **You have a three percent approval rating . . .
Saddam Hussein has an eight.
How does that make you feel that ninety-seven
percent of America hates you.**

Linda:

It feels like high school.

COLIN QUINN

UPDATE: PAULA JONES

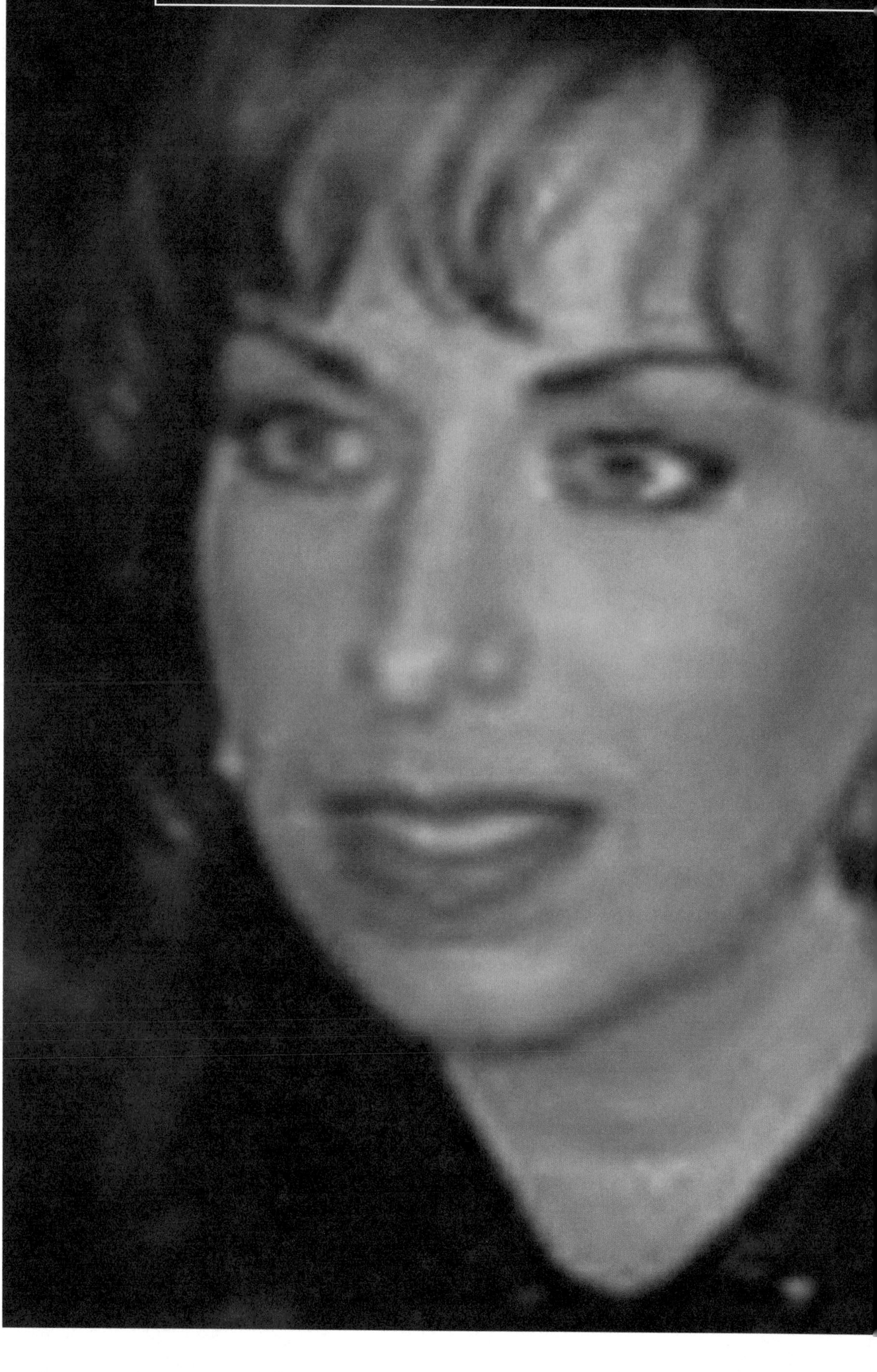

President Clinton agreed yesterday to pay Paula Jones **eight hundred and fifty thousand dollars** to drop her sexual harassment lawsuit, making it the most money a HILLBILLY has gotten since Buddy Ebsen was shooting at some food.

Cop: **This is gonna be some line up, Briggs.**

Cop: **This is some case, Donovan. "William Jefferson Clinton vs. Paula Jones."**

Cop: **You really think she can ID him by his you-know-what**

Cop: **That's what the lady says.**

JIM BREUER MOLLY SHANNON CHERI OTERI CHRIS KATTAN TIM MEADOWS MARK McKINNEY NORM MACDONALD

LINE UP COLD OPEN

Paula Jones: **Oh my dear...This is like the world's worst Chippendale's show.**

Cop: **Ms. Jones, you know why you're here. Do any of these five sets of genitalia look familiar?**

Lawyer: **Take your time, Paula. Think back to that day...**

(PAULA LOOKS CLOSELY)

Paula: **Man, this is difficult. This all happened over ten years ago. A lot can change on a man in ten years, a lot of wear and tear...Well, it's not the black guy...**

(CLARENCE THOMAS STEPS BACKWARD) Clarence: **Bet you wish it was, baby.**

Paula: **And it's not lefty . . .** (AL GORE STEPS BACK) Al: **Thank God!**

Paula: **And that one on the right — the hair is jet black, but it's obviously a dye job.**

(BOB DOLE STEPS BACK) Bob: **I'll give you a dye job, you dirty tramp.**

Paula: **So it's definitely one of the two fat guys . . .**

UPDATE FEATURE: VERNON JORDAN

Colin: ...Over the past year, Clinton confidante Vernon Jordan has emerged as a major player in one of the most important events in recent history: The impeachment of the President. Here now to discuss his Senate deposition earlier this week is Vernon Jordan.

Vernon: **Good evening, Colin. And thank you for extending this invitation to me.**

Colin: **Vernon, we all know you're some kind of lawyer, and that you're a friend of the President's, and that you may be one of the most powerful men in Washington. But I have to ask: What exactly do you do?**

Vernon: (CHUCKLES, SMUG) **Well, Colin, I'm that rarest of species known as a Beltway Insider. A man behind the scenes. By day I lunch with kings!** WINKINGLY **By night I dine with queens! What's more, I always have a perfect dimple in my tie!**

Colin: **But, what does that really mean?**

Vernon: **That I'm a player on the scene!**

Colin: **Still, I've heard all that before!**

Vernon: **Oh, but wait — I'm much, much more!** (MUSIC: BOUNCING PIANO)

LIKE REX HARRISON IN "MY FAIR LADY"

I'm an attorney and a lobbyist, an essayist, a hobbyist! An amateur ornithologist! Why, I wear many hats! FLAMBOYANTLY DONS A BOWLER **I'm a gadabout, a ne'er-do-well! A rake, a rogue, a fancy swell! A modern-day-style William Tell! I'm really all of thaaaaaaaat...**

TIM JUMPS IN FRONT OF UPDATE DESK, PRODUCES A CANE AND STARTS SINGING

WHILE THE SENATE SITS DEBATING I GO OUT PROMENADING WITH A SMART-SET LASS OR LAD! I'M CHUMMY WITH THE PRESIDENT A LOCAL D.C. RESIDENT I CANNOT STAND A BOOR OR CAD! WHERE CHAMPAGNE CORKS ARE POPPING AND "TRAY BONE MOE" ARE SWAPPING YOU'LL FIND ME IN WITH THE CROWD! WHEN A LADY NEEDS A SQUIRE OR A GOOD FRIEND NEEDS A LIAR JUST SAY MY NAME OUT LOUD! AND I'LL TIP MY HAT TO YOU SIR AS A GENTLEMAN SHOULD DO SIR

FOR I...
AM VERNON JORDAN

HORATIO, ANA, PARNELL, AND MOLLY, IN EDWARDIAN CLOTHES, WOMEN WITH PARASOLS, STROLL ON AND FLANK TIM

All: **HE'LL TIE HIS TIE PUT ON HIS SPATS IN BARELY TWENTY SECONDS FLAT HE'S A TROUBLE-SHOOTING MAN ABOUT THE TOWN**

Vernon: OPERA TICKETS   YES INDEED
A SUMMER JOB   FOR FRIENDS IN NEED?
LOOK NO FURTHER   GOOD OLD VERNON IS AROUND

Ana: I FEAR I'VE BEEN INDICTED!
Vernon: WHY THAT WRONG WILL SOON BE RIGHTED!
Parnell: I'M A LITTLE SHORT ON CASH!
Vernon: IT'LL BE THERE IN A FLASH!
Molly: WE NEED A FOURTH FOR TENNIS!
Vernon: ON THE COURT I AM A MENACE!
Horatio: IT SEEMS YOU NEVER FAIL TO PLEASE!

Vernon: SLOWING DOWN AND I EVEN SPEAK CHINESE!... THEY ALL JOIN ARMS BEHIND TIM

All: 'CAUSE HE'S THE...
PROBLEM-SOLVING
WORLD-REVOLVING
EXPEDITIOUS
MERETRICIOUS
COURTROOM HANDY
DAPPER DANDY
CONFETTI FALLS
VER-NON...JORRRR-DANNNNN!

Vernon: That's me!

149

Hillary: **Bill, I'm kind of busy. Is this really important?**

Bill: **Well, kinda. A lot of people have been asking about the health care reform package.**

Hillary: **What about it?**

Bill: **Well, they wanna know what it's going to include and when it's going to be made public.**

Hillary: **Well, at this point, Bill, I honestly haven't the faintest idea.**

Bill: **Right. Un huh. Well, you think you'll have it ready by Fall?**

Hillary: **Truthfully? I don't think so.**

Bill: **Well, is there anything definite you can tell me about it?**

Hillary: (MATTER-OF-FACTLY) **We know it's going to require a big tax increase.**

Bill: **Un huh. I figured that. Anything else?**

Hillary: **Free needles for addicts.** Bill: **Un huh.**

Hillary: **You won't be able to choose your own doctor. We know that.**

Bill: **Is that about it?** Hillary: **So far.** Bill: **Oh boy.**

(INTERCOM) **Mr. President. Senator Dole is here. He says it's important.**

Bill: **Fine. Fine, send him in.** (TO JAN) **Now, Hillary, we need Bob Dole. So let's put on the charm.**

Hillary: **Don't worry. I know just what to do.**

(DAN AYKROYD, AS DOLE, ENTERS) Bob: **Hello, Hillary, Bill.**

Hillary: (EXTENDING HER HAND) **Hi, Bob. Good to see you.**

Bill: **Bob, have a seat. What can I do for you?**

Bob: **Well Bill, I thought perhaps...it would be best if we could talk...in private.**

Hillary: **This is private.**

Bob: **I was hoping that Bill and I might...**

Hillary:

I happen to be co-President of the United States.

Anything you say to my husband, you can say to me.

Monica: **Well, it was that way with me and the President. But my friends would all be saying, "Monica, are you guys gonna get married? He is so interesting and so gorgeous!"**

And I'd be like, "Hello!

A, He's got a wife,

and **B**,
I don't even like
gorgeous guys!"
And it's true.
I don't.

In my whole life,

I only had one really gorgeous boyfriend...

my high school boyfriend. His dad's company made like, all the lenses or something they use on movie cameras? So like, any movie or TV show, his dad made the lenses. **They lived in Bel Air.** Anyway, he was like scary cute.

I mean, you couldn't even look at him. He was like, that hot! And my friends would be like, "Monica, Elliot is so gorgeous." And I'm like, "But I don't even like gorgeous guys." And they'd be like, "Well, they sure love you!"

UPDATE: HILLARY & PALESTINE

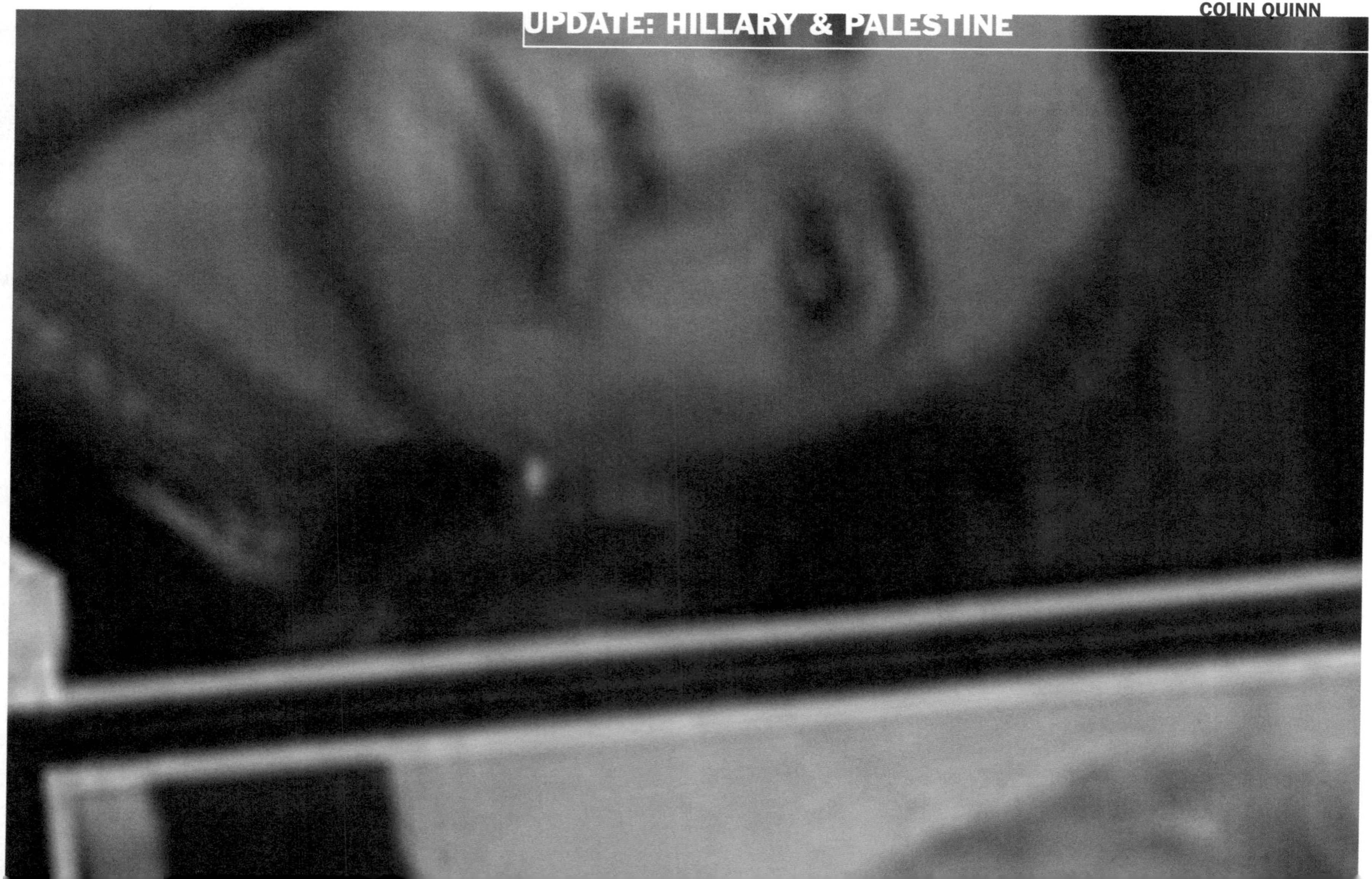

Hillary Clinton said this week that Palestinians should have their own free state. The President pointed out that the statement didn't reflect official government policy, but added if they wanted to become a free state, he and Hillary would be glad to broker the land deal.

A spokesman for the First Lady said that her views are "personal" and in no way reflect the views of the President...

much like their wedding vows.

The White House
had no

KEVIN NEALON

UPDATE: NO COMMENT

comment.

About the Compilers

MICHAEL SHOEMAKER is a co-producer of "Saturday Night Live."

SCOTT WEINSTEIN is the Weekend Update Coordinator for the show.